Contents

Some words are shown in bold, **like this**. You can find out what they mean by looking in the glossary.

What is a plane?

A plane is a machine that flies through the air. Some planes carry passengers. Some planes carry **goods** called cargo. People often fly planes for fun.

These pilots are enjoying the open air in their private plane.

REVISED AND UPDATED

es

le

Heinemann
LIBRARY

www.heinemann.co.uk
Visit our website to find out more information about Heinemann Library books.

To order:
 Phone 44 (0) 1865 888066
 Send a fax to 44 (0) 1865 314091
 Visit the Heinemann Bookshop at www.heinemann.co.uk to browse our catalogue and order online.

First published in Great Britain by Heinemann Library,
Halley Court, Jordan Hill, Oxford OX2 8EJ, part of Pearson Education.
Heinemann is a registered trademark of Pearson Education Ltd.

Editorial: Diyan Leake and Kristen Truhlar
Design: Kimberley R. Miracle and Ray Hendren
Picture research: Erica Martin
Production: Julie Carter

Originated by Chroma Graphics (Overseas) Pte Ltd
Printed and bound in China by South China Printing Co. Ltd

ISBN 978 0 4310 8700 9 (hardback)
12 11 10 09 08
10 9 8 7 6 5 4 3 2 1

ISBN 978 0 4310 8710 8 (paperback)
12 11 10 09
10 9 8 7 6 5 4 3 2

British Library Cataloguing in Publication Data
Oxlade, Chris
Transport Around the World: Planes

A full catalogue record for this book is available from the British Library

Acknowledgements
The publishers would like to thank the following for permission to reproduce photographs: AirTeam Images 2007 pp. **13** (Eric Fortin), **25** (Colin Work); Alamy p. **24** (Steve Mansfield-Devine); Corbis p. **21** (George Hall); Getty Images/AFP p. **15**; Photodisc pp. **23**, **29**; Quadrant pp. **5** (Jeremy Hoare), **7** (R. Shaw), 12 (Erik Simonsen), **16** (Mark Wagner), **17** (LG Photo), **18** (Anthony R. Dalton), **19** (Paul Phelan), **22** (Tony Hobbs), **27** (Tony Hobbs); Quadrant/Flight pp. **6**, **8**, **9**, **11**, **20**, **26**; The Stock Market p. **10** (Russell Munson); Tony Stone Images pp. **14** (Alan Smith), **28** (World Perspectives); Trip p. **4** (Malcolm Fife).

Cover photograph of a jet plane reproduced with permission of Getty Images/Science Faction (Paul Bowen).

The publishers would like to thank Carrie Reiling for her assistance in the publication of this book.

Every effort has been made to contact copyright holders of any material reproduced in this book. Any omissions will be rectified in subsequent printings if notice is given to the publishers.

Pilots need to know how high they are and how fast they are going.

The person who flies a plane is called the **pilot**. The pilot controls the take-off and landing, and **steers** the plane through the air. Some pilots have computers to help them fly the plane.

How planes work

This small plane can hold about 10 passengers.

Wings keep a plane in the air. As the plane flies along, some air rushes under the wings and some air rushes over the wings. The air pushes the wings upwards.

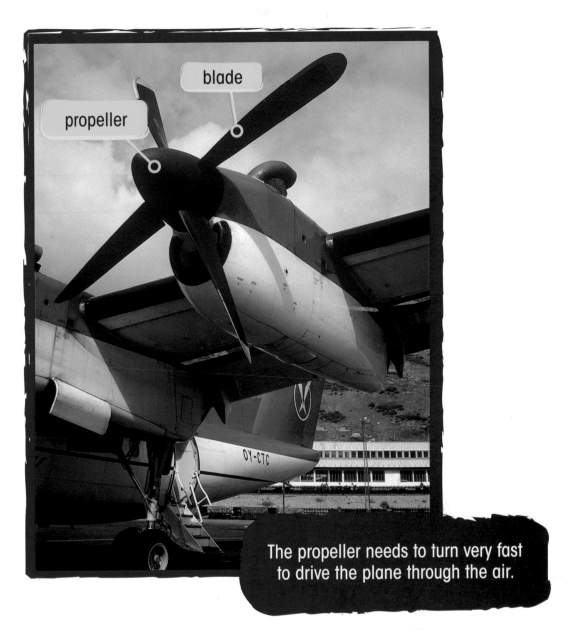

propeller

blade

The propeller needs to turn very fast to drive the plane through the air.

Engines power a plane through the air. This engine makes a **propeller** spin round. The propeller **blades** push air backwards, which makes the plane go forwards.

Old planes

The first plane to fly using an **engine** was Flyer 1. It was built by two American brothers in 1903. They were called Orville and Wilbur Wright.

The Flyer 1 got into the air for 59 seconds on the fourth try.

People flew on this kind of airliner around 80 years ago.

An **airliner** is a plane that carries passengers. Early airliners were slow and very noisy. They were not very comfortable.

Where planes are used

All planes fly in the air. On long flights, **jet airliners** fly about 10 kilometres (6 miles) above the ground. Some smaller planes fly closer to the ground.

Jet airliners fly above the clouds long distances between cities.

The planes on the ground here are getting ready to fly. The plane in the air is about to land.

You catch a plane at an airport. Airports are busy places with many planes taking off and landing. Planes take off and land on a **runway**.

Airliners

Passenger planes are called **airliners**. The Boeing 747 is a huge airliner. It is sometimes called the jumbo **jet**.

The jumbo jet usually flies between continents.

During the flight the passengers can eat a meal. Some jumbo jets even have video games in the backs of the seats for passengers. Jumbo jets fly on long journeys all over the world.

There are seats for hundreds of people inside a jumbo jet.

Amazing planes

Supersonic planes fly through the air faster than sound. Sound speeds along at 1,250 kilometres (775 miles) per hour. Supersonic planes go faster than this! Concorde was a supersonic **airliner**.

Concorde flew from Europe to New York, in the United States.

The first trial flight of the Airbus A830 was in 2006.

The Airbus A380 is the biggest airliner in the world. Its two decks have seats for 555 passengers. It is made to fly very long distances.

Cargo planes

A cargo plane is a plane that carries **goods** or cargo. Inside the plane is a cargo **hold**. During the flight, boxes are tied down to stop them moving about in the hold.

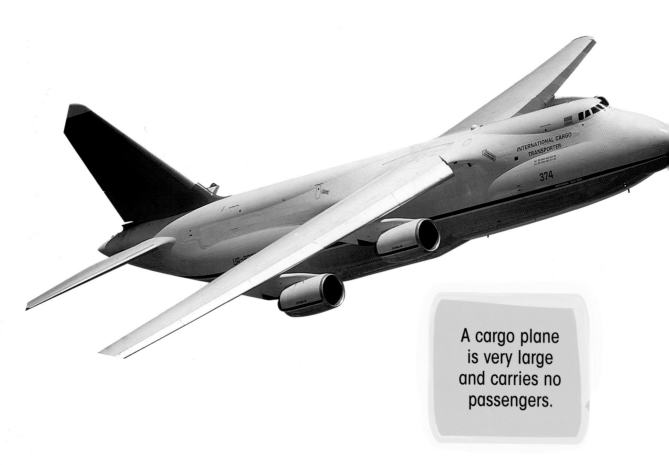

A cargo plane is very large and carries no passengers.

Cargo needs to be carefully packed and loaded into the plane.

cargo

A cargo plane has a huge door. It opens wide to let large pieces of cargo into the plane. A special truck lifts the cargo up to the door.

Seaplanes

A seaplane is a plane that takes off and lands on water. Seaplanes use the water instead of a **runway**. They are useful for flying to places where there is nowhere to build a runway.

Seaplanes can land in areas that cannot be reached by car or train.

A seaplane has two floats instead of wheels. The floats let the seaplane skim across the water for take-off and landing.

Seaplanes are like normal planes on a pair of water skis.

floats

Vertical take-off

Some planes, such as the Harrier jet, can take off by flying straight up into the air instead of using a **runway**. The Harrier can also fly like a normal plane.

The Harrier jet is useful when there is not a lot of space to take off and land.

The power that pushes the Harrier jet upward also moves it quickly through the air.

nozzles

The Harrier has powerful **jet engines**. For take-off and landing, the engine's **nozzles** point downwards. For flying along, they point backwards.

Gliders

A glider is a plane without an **engine**. A glider is towed into the air by another plane and glides slowly back to the ground. People fly gliders for fun.

A ride in a glider can be relaxing while drifting in the air through the countryside.

Gliders use the movement of the wind to go forward and to change direction.

A glider has long, thin wings. They keep the glider up as it flies slowly along. The glider's smooth shape lets it cut easily through the air.

23

Microlights

A microlight is a tiny plane. It can only carry one or two people. The microlight's wing is made of a plastic sheet fixed to thin metal tubes.

A microlight has a small engine and small propellers to keep it in the air.

The wing design and the pilot's skill keep this low-powered plane in the air.

The **pilot's** seat hangs underneath the wing. The pilot **steers** the plane up and down, and to the left and right, by moving a bar that is attached to the wing.

Fighter planes

Fighter planes are used in wars to fight other planes in the air. They also attack targets on the ground. Fighters are small, fast planes that can turn very quickly.

This fighter plane is known as the Eurofighter Typhoon.

missile

Fighters attack enemy planes and targets with **missiles** and guns. The missiles are fixed under the fighter's wings. To fire a missile, the **pilot** presses a button in the **cockpit**.

A fighter plane must be very fast.

Space shuttles

A space shuttle is a plane that goes into space. It takes off like a rocket. Booster rockets give it an extra push.

space shuttle

The shuttle is attached to containers of fuel to help it fly into space.

When its job in space is finished, the shuttle returns to Earth. It glides down and lands on a **runway** like an ordinary plane. Parachutes help it to slow down.

The space shuttle lands just like an ordinary plane. It needs an extra-long runway.

parachute

Timeline

1783   A hot-air balloon made by the Montgolfier brothers in France carries people into the air for the first time.

1852   The first **airship** takes off in France with its builder Henry Giffard.

1903   In the United States, the Wright brothers take off in their aeroplane Flyer 1. It is the first aeroplane with an **engine** to fly properly.

1933   American pilot Wiley Post flies around the world on his own. The 25,000-kilometre (15,500-mile) flight takes nearly eight days.

1969   The first Boeing 747 jumbo **jet** takes off for a test flight. Passengers first flew in a 747 in 1970.

1969   In France, the supersonic **airliner** Concorde flies for the first time. It starts carrying passengers in 1976. Concorde's last flight is in 2003.

1981   A space shuttle takes off for the first time from Kennedy Space Center in the United States.

2001   The Global Hawk flies from Edwards Air Force Base in the United States to Australia non-stop without a pilot. This is the longest flight ever by a pilotless plane and takes 23 hours and 23 minutes.

2005   American pilot Steve Fossett completes the first non-stop plane flight around the world on his own. The trip takes him 67 hours and 2 minutes.

Glossary

airliner   large plane that carries passengers

airship   balloon with an engine to move it along

blade   one of the long, flat pieces on a propeller

cockpit   space at the front of a plane where the pilot sits

engine   machine that powers movement using fuel. A plane's engine moves the plane along.

goods   things that people buy and sell

hold   part of the plane where goods and luggage are kept

jet   a type of engine. A jet engine sends out a stream of gas backwards that pushes a plane forwards.

missile   machine that flies straight through the air and explodes when it reaches its target

nozzle   hole where gas and hot air come out of an engine

pilot   person who flies the plane

propeller   part of a plane that is attached to the engine and turns to make the plane move

runway   long, straight strip of ground where planes take off and land

steer   guide the direction of the plane

Find Out More

Great Inventions: The Airplane, Julie Sinclair (Capstone, 2003).

Machines at Work: Airplane, Caroline Bingham (DK, 2006).

Oxford Reds: Aeroplane, Jan Mark (Oxford University Press, 2003).

Start to Finish: From Metal to Airplane, Robin Nelson (Lerner, 2004).

Usborne Beginners: Planes, Kamini Khanduri (Usborne, 2003).

Index

DK READERS

BEGINNING
TO READ
1

Submarines
and Submersibles

Written by Deborah Lock

DK

A Dorling Kindersley Book

Down, down, down.
The submersible
[sub-MER-suh-bull]
dives under the sea.

A Note to Parents and Teachers

DK READERS is a compelling reading programme for children, designed in conjunction with leading literacy experts, including Cliff Moon M.Ed., Honorary Fellow of the University of Reading. Cliff Moon has spent many years as a teacher and teacher educator specializing in reading and has written more than 160 books for children and teachers. He is series editor to Collins Big Cat.

Beautiful illustrations and superb full-colour photographs combine with engaging, easy-to-read stories to offer a fresh approach to each subject in the series. Each DK READER is guaranteed to capture a child's interest while developing his or her reading skills, general knowledge, and love of reading.

The five levels of DK READERS are aimed at different reading abilities, enabling you to choose the books that are exactly right for your child:

Pre-level 1: Learning to read
Level 1: Beginning to read
Level 2: Beginning to read alone
Level 3: Reading alone
Level 4: Proficient readers

The "normal" age at which a child begins to read can be anywhere from three to eight years old. Adult participation through the lower levels is very helpful for providing encouragement, discussing storylines and sounding out unfamiliar words.

No matter which level you select, you can be sure that you are helping your child learn to read, then read to learn!

DK

LONDON, NEW YORK, MUNICH,
MELBOURNE and DELHI

Series Editor Deborah Lock
Senior Art Editor Sonia Moore
Production Georgina Hayworth
Picture Researcher Debra Weatherley
DTP Designer Emma Hansen
Jacket Designer Simon Oon

Reading Consultant
Cliff Moon, M.Ed.

Published in Great Britain by
Dorling Kindersley Limited,
80 Strand, London WC2R 0RL

Copyright © 2007 Dorling Kindersley Limited
A Penguin Company

2 4 6 8 10 9 7 5 3 1
RD130 - 11/06

ISBN: 978-1-4053-1941-6

Colour reproduction by Colourscan, Singapore
Printed and bound in China by L Rex Printing Co., Ltd.

The publisher would like to thank the following for their
kind permission to reproduce their photographs:
Position key: a-above; b-below/bottom; c-centre;
l-left; r-right; t-top
2005 BAE Systems: 3b, 20-21c; Corbis: Mark Cooper
29r, 32cla; Roger Ressmeyer 26; Getty Images: Torsten
Blackwood / AFP 15b; Randy Olson / National
Geographic 18c; Jeff Rotman / Iconica 16-17c; Brian
Skerry 12-13c; Kurt Vinion 22b, 32tl; Image Quest
Marine: James D. Watt 10-11c; Jeff Rotman / jeffrotman.
com: 2tr, 2t, 4c, 5b, 6l, 6-7c, 8-9c, 11t, 14c, 32clb;
Navsource: Brian Nokell / US Navy Photo 24-25c, 30b,
32cl; Larry Smith / Defence Visual Information Center
22-23c, 27t, 28-29c; US Navy Photo 1br; Perry Slingsby
Systems: 2br, 16t, 16b; Photolibrary: Purestock 30-31c;
SMD Hydrovision: 2cr, 17cr; Woods Hole
Oceanographic Instititution: 19b
All other images © Dorling Kindersley
For further information see: www.dkimages.com

Discover more at
www.dk.com

Contents

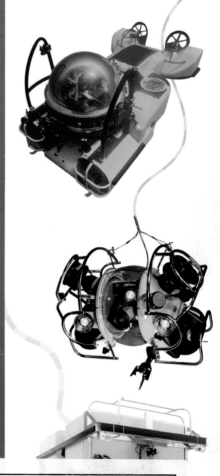

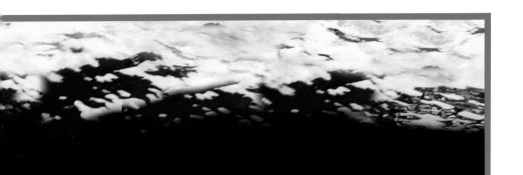

A submersible is a craft used
for short trips deep underwater.
This submersible has
three people on board.

Jim, the pilot, steers
the submersible.
The computer screen
shows him where
to go.

computer
screen

Mark and Paul
look out
of the window.
They want to find out
about the sea floor.

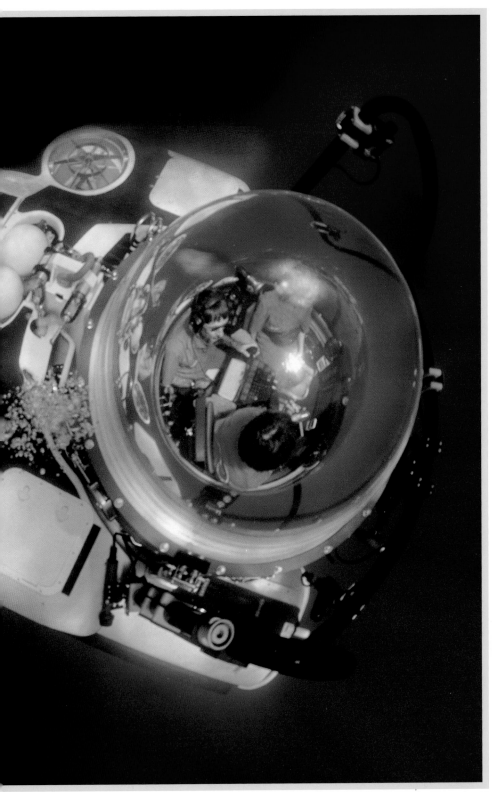

The submersible
reaches the sea floor.
The crew watches the sea animals.
"I can see an octopus," says Mark.
"Let's take a video of it."

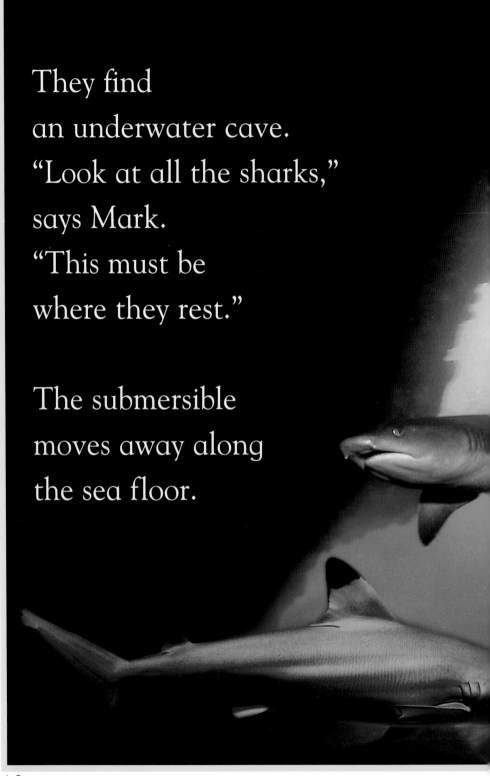

They find
an underwater cave.
"Look at all the sharks,"
says Mark.
"This must be
where they rest."

The submersible
moves away along
the sea floor.

A strange shape appears
in front of them.
"What's that?" asks Jim.

submarine

"It looks like the wreck
of an old war submarine
[sub-MUH-reen]," says Paul.
"We'd better be going," says Jim.
"The water's getting rough."

Jim steers the submersible
to the surface.
A crane lifts it out of the water.

"We can send the underwater
robot to look at the wreck,"
says Paul.

Robot submersibles,
or ROVs, are used when
the water is dangerous.
They are used to
explore the sea floor
and wrecks.

ROVs can also be used
to lay cables and mend
pipes deep underwater.

The ROV is lowered
into the water.
It has a cable line
linking it
to the ship.

Jim controls the ROV
from the ship and steers it
around the wreck.
It sends back pictures of
the submarine.

Modern submarines can carry
more than 120 people.
They are often used for
long trips underwater.

Many submarines are painted
black so it is hard to see them
in the dark water.

This submarine is docked
in a harbour.
The crew gets the submarine
ready to leave.

hatch

Then they climb inside.
"Close the hatches,"
orders the captain.

The submarine moves away
from the dock.
Out at sea, the submarine
dives below the waves.
It will be at sea for three months.

The crew takes turns eating,
working and sleeping.
Their beds are bunks.

Some members of the crew
work in the control room.
After three months underwater,
they take the submarine
up to the surface.

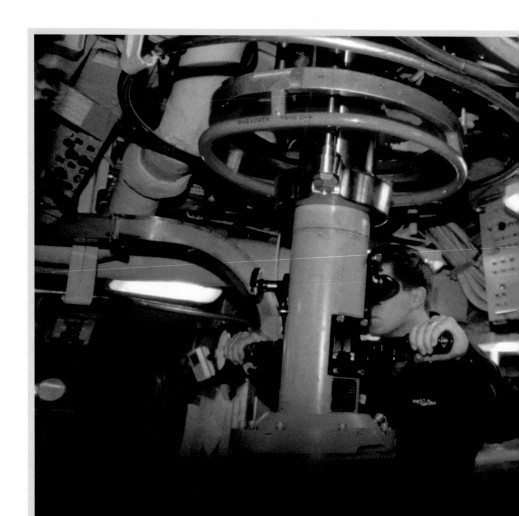

The captain needs to make sure
it is safe to surface.
The periscopes [PE-ri-skohps]
are raised just above the water.

periscope

The men look through
the eyepieces.
The mirrors inside the periscopes
show them what is on the surface.

The men can see the coast.

They are almost home.

"Surface," the captain orders.

Up, up, up.

sail

The submarine's sail appears first.
The submarine makes a big wave
as it rises.
SWOOSH!

Glossary

Computer screen a surface that shows pictures

Hatch an opening used to get into a submarine

Periscope a long tube used to see above the water

Sail the raised part of a submarine

Submarine a craft that can travel underwater